STATION ZED

Books by Tom Sleigh

POETRY ↝

Station Zed
Army Cats
Space Walk
Bula Matari/Smasher of Rocks (Limited Edition)
Far Side of the Earth
The Dreamhouse
The Chain
Waking
After One

ESSAYS ↝

Interview with a Ghost

TRANSLATION ↝

Herakles by Euripides

STATION ZED

POEMS

TOM SLEIGH

Graywolf Press

This publication is made possible, in part, by the voters of Minnesota through a Minnesota State Arts Board Operating Support grant, thanks to a legislative appropriation from the arts and cultural heritage fund, and through grants from the National Endowment for the Arts and the Wells Fargo Foundation Minnesota. Significant support has also been provided by Target, the McKnight Foundation, Amazon.com, and other generous contributions from foundations, corporations, and individuals. To these organizations and individuals we offer our heartfelt thanks.

Published by Graywolf Press
250 Third Avenue North, Suite 600
Minneapolis, Minnesota 55401

www.graywolfpress.org

Published in the United States of America

ISBN 978-1-55597-698-9

2 4 6 8 9 7 5 3 1
First Graywolf Printing, 2015

Library of Congress Control Number: 2014948532

Cover design: Kyle G. Hunter

Cover photo: TJ Blackwell, *Sulaymaniyah City Limits, Iraq*. Used with the permission of Getty Images.

For Sarah

Contents

Let the smells of mint go heady and defenceless
Like inmates liberated in that yard.
Like the disregarded ones we turned against
Because we'd failed them by our disregard.

> ∼ Seamus Heaney, "Mint"

STATION ZED

I

Homage to Mary Hamilton

I'm driving past discarded tires,
      the all night carwash dreams
near Green-Wood Cemetery where
      the otherworld of Queens

puts out trash—trash of Murder, Inc.,
      trash of heartbeat
in recycled newspapers where
      Romeo and Juliet meet.

So much thorny underbrush,
      so much ice overgrowing
my windshield until frost shields a buck
      behind a billboard forest

selling someone's half-dressed daughter.
      She melts into the defroster
roaring like the rich guys' helicopters
      at the Wall Street heliport,

rotoring down through skyscrapers
      where torchsong lipstick smears
onto a handkerchief and starched collar.
      But in my face snow blizzards

up from sixteen-wheelers and
      three crows clot against limbs
downswooping, omen of the augurs
      that steers the desperate lovers

to a crossroads, right here. And where mobsters
              and suicides lie buried
and the radio breaks into a ballad
              of Mary Hamilton's fair body,

but who's tied it in her apron
              and thrown it in the sea,
I'm the quake and shortlived quiver,
              the laughter and fractured tale

of her night in the laigh cellar
              with the hichest Stewart of a'.
Oh, she's washed the Queen's feet
              and gently laid her down

but a' the thanks she's gotten this night's
              to be hanged in Edinbro' town.
I'm sitting behind the wheel
              of our mutual desire

when the heel comes off her shoe
              on the Parliament stair
and lang or she cam down again
              she was condemned to dee:

but the instant the news comes on
              and drones spy down
on our compulsions, her hands
              under my hands wrestle

on the wheel as my foot taps
              the brakes, her foot the gas
when out of the gliding dark
              I spot his velvet rack.

Last night there were four Toms,
      today they'll be but three:
there was Tom Fool, Sweet Tooth Tom,
      Tom the Bomb, and me.

A Short History of Communism
and the Enigma of Surplus Value

My grandfather on his Allis Chalmers WC tractor, a natural
    Communist
who hated Communism, is an example of Marx's proletariat,
though nothing near in his own mind what Marx meant by the masses—
musing in his messianic beard, Marx intuited the enigma
of surplus value that my grandfather understood
from a cutter bar and threshing drum driving into the future
as the combine harvester, thus increasing the bushels
he could harvest each hour, thus increasing his hourly productivity
for each minute expended of muscle foot pound power—
but Marx didn't foresee, exactly, that the tractor
would develop into a techno Taj Majal, complete
with safety glass cab, filtered AC, a surround sound system
that could rival Carnegie Hall or blast Led Zeppelin
at decibels that left your ears dazed, easily drowning out
the invincible tractor's roar—and the hydraulics, so swift
you could lift the discs with a touch—and all this,
in the old man's mind, contrasting with the tractor
he put me on to learn, a four stroke with a crank you had to turn,
cursing and turning until it shook itself and shook itself
like a drunk with the DTs, until clearing the mystification
of its hallucinated roles, the tractor refused to sing the song
of its own reification and hiccuped and lurched into the real.
I'd climb onto the iron seat with a threadbare pad
that made my ass sweat, a jug of iced tea wrapped in burlap,
a bandana knotted to keep dust out of my mouth, goggles
snapped onto my face like an ideologue's dream so that I saw
the fields foursquare as I contour-plowed acre after acre
unfolding before me with such dialectical rigor

that the ground of being would hold still forever, never blowing
into reactions of horizon-shrouding dust whipped by the hot winds
    of contingency.
Such a theory Marx made to argue the enigma into sense—
and not just for himself but for the eponymous masses!
But my grandfather's big nose and wary drinker's eyes keep breaking
    through
the mask and posing an alternative enigma: what if his surplus value
led him not to solidarity with the worker but made him into a Kulak
who must be killed? So the locomotive pulls out
of the Finland Station, so the colors red and white
make uniforms for themselves: Lenin. Trotsky.
Moth-eaten Czar Nicholas. Technicolor Rasputin.
The ones who stood in front of Kresty Prison
for three hundred hours. But the colors saw them coming—
and wore the ones who wore them to rags.
But fast forward a hundred years, my grandfather dead for fifty,
and there, in a window on Fifth Avenue, the enigma
hides itself in the headless, sexless torso of a mannequin
as a fly lands on its finger, the window shattering
to a thousand windows in the lenses of its eyes.
And all the while the enigma, like the embalmed body of Lenin,
keeps on breathing through his waxworks face.

The Parallel Cathedral

1

The cathedral being built
around our split level house was so airy, it stretched
so high it was like a cloud of granite
and marble light the house rose up inside.

At the time I didn't notice masons laying courses
of stone ascending, flying buttresses
pushing back forces that would have crushed our flimsy wooden
    beams.
But the hammering and singing of the guilds went on

outside my hearing, the lancets' stained glass
telling how a tree rose up from Jesse's loins whose
flower was Jesus staring longhaired from our bathroom wall

where I wanted to ask if this was how he looked for real,
slender, neurasthenic, itching for privacy
as the work went on century after century.

2

Fog in cherry trees, deer strapped
to bumpers, fresh snow marked
by dog piss shining frozen in the day made
a parallel cathedral unseen but intuited

by eyes that took it in and went on to the next
thing and the next as if unbuilding
a cathedral was the work
that really mattered—not knocking

it down, which was easy—
but taking it apart stone
by stone until all

that's left is the cathedral's
outline coming in and out of limbo
in the winter sun.

3

All through childhood on eternal sick-day afternoons,
I lived true to my name, piling dominoes
into towers, fingering the white dots like the carpenter Thomas
putting fingertips into the nail-holes of his master's hands.

A builder and a doubter. Patron saint of all believers
in what's really there every time you look:
black-scabbed cherry trees unleafed in winter,
the irrigation ditch that overflows at the back

of the house, chainlink of the schoolyard
where frozen footsteps in the snow
criss-cross and doubleback. And now the shroud falls away

and the wound under his nipple seeps fresh blood.
And when Jesus says, *Whither I go you know,*
Thomas says, *We know not . . . how can we know the way?*

Songs for the Cold War

1/ BOOMERANG

The sidelong whiplash of his arm sent the boomerang
soaring, pushing the sky to the horizon
until the blade just hung there, a black slash on the sun

so far away it seemed not to move at all
before it came whirling back larger and larger:
would it hit him, would he die—and you ducked down,

terrified, clinging to his thigh, its deathspin
slowing as it coptered softly down and he snatched it
from the air. How you loved that rush of fear,

both wanting and not wanting him to feel how hard
you clung, just the same as when he'd float you
weightless across the pond while waves slapped

and shushed and bickered, his breath loud in your ear . . .
and after he dried you off, he'd lift you onto his shoulders
and help you shove your head through a hole in the sky.

2/ BIKE

The first time I let loose the handlebars
and the bike steered itself, fat tires balancing
on their spinning hubs, the sky came closer

to the ground, the mountain slope receding
at the far end of the street was an exercise
in three-point perspective. One point was the bike

carrrying me along through an infinitely
narrowing alley of shrinking box elder trees,
the second was a bird's eye foreshortening the slope,

while the third loomed way up high where blinking
satellites passed by, some shadowy sky-presence
that knew depth and height together,

knew my knees pumping the pedals and my hands
down at my sides countering the breeze in the *now*
now now now of my swaying in the balance.

3/ BOMB SHELTER

There was a Bay, there was a Pig, there was a Missile.
There was a Screen, there was a Beard talking loud talk
in Spanish, there was the Screen in English calling him Dictator.

There was the floor of the room, a checkerboard
of brown and white squares, there were Moves
that were the right ones, and Moves that meant War.

There was a Bomb Shelter rumored to have been built
by a church elder across town. There was Radiation
that let you see the bones of your foot in the shoestore.

There was a Hot War at school where mean kids beat up
Weegee Johnson's brother, and there was a Cold War
that meant everyone would die. The cat kneaded

your mother's lap. The dog let loose a growling sigh.
The Pig kept squealing in the Bay, the Missile sweated,
the Screen counted down to zero and turned static.

4/ DUST RAG

What was Jesus writing in the dust? The magic hand
of Jesus writing something down? Maybe what would happen next
to you and her as she sat there beside you on the naugahyde

and cried and Jesus kept on writing until a great stone
rolled down on him from Heaven and crushed him?
The Bible didn't tell you so but Jesus was the stone, Jesus

was the President riding in the car, Jesus was the holes
in the President's throat and head, Jesus was the television
floating down from out of Heaven that brought to you

the bullets and the horses dragging the coffin
to be buried in the red letters of Jesus' words
bleeding on the black and white skull of the President.

She cried on the couch and you sat there watching
Jesus writing in the dust like the dust you wrote
your name in before the dust rag came along and wiped it out.

5/ MARBLES

"Elephant stomp" meant you stomped your marble
with your heel until it was buried level with the earth.
If you felt brave enough you played for "keepsies,"

if you doubted your concentration you called
"quitsies" and if you wanted to come close
or get away you called "giant steps." Contingency

dictated "bombsies" when you stood up straight
and from the level of your eye looking right down
to your target you called out "bombs away."

No one liked to lose a "clearie" or a "steelie"
and nothing teachers said about fair play
reduced the sting and shame and anger:

your bag's size waxed and waned, adrenaline
pumped all recess, you were acquisitive,
sharp-eyed, pitting vision against gain and loss.

6/ SHOOTER

"Upsy elbows and straights" meant you had to keep
your arm straight and with your shooting hand
snug against the inside of your elbow you'd cock

your thumb, shooter gritty with dirt, and take aim
at your opponent's marble. Calculations went on
that made time and space purely malleable,

sudden vectors of intention taking over
from the sun so you were seeing it as if
foreknown, though the sharp little click glass on glass

put to the test Zeno's paradox: in the just
before not quite yet never to be realized
consummation, you grew a long white beard,

you outlived the earth and all the stars and never
would you die as long as you kept measuring
the space between the cat's eye and your eye.

The Craze

What could I say, a laborer, to the overseas geniuses?
That my father fought their war against the Japanese?

That the leisure class I served I aspired to, so I could join
the high G of the cello floating off, slowly vanishing

in a *pianissimo fermata?* Then nothing more,
silence and night? But this was California,

and soon the heat pump and water filter
would strain the water to such a blueness and temperature

that acid-washed LA would go swimming night and day,
the blue havens built by alambristas, union bricklayers, unskilled
    juvies

teaching me the Faustian accounting
of my employer, Bob "Just Call Me a Genius" Harrington:

Screw 'em out of this, screw 'em out of that,
but sweep up your mess and you'll get

away with murder. Sucking up the slurry of cement
and sand, the hose pulsed in the pit

of the parvenu, the ingenue, the Hollywood producers
and Van Nuys GM bosses whose assembly-line crews

riveted my beat-up Firebird's body, Wolfman Jack's XERB
taking *another little piece of my heart now, baby,*

as I sprayed gunite on rebar ribs and the air compressor
pounded like the other *Firebird:* Stravinsky taking his temperature

in West Hollywood, Schoenberg watering his lawn in Brentwood,
Mann perched above the waves in Pacific Palisades

had also perused catalogs weighing concrete vs. vinyl
as blast caps detonated in holes the demmies drilled

and ash sifted down over my face and shoulders
to post-war twelve tone assaulting my ears.

But while I and my transistor radio worked ten hour days,
my father dreamt our own little South Seas grotto:

every weekend we rose to the promise of chlorination
as he and "us boys" dug trenches for our water lines,

hacked away the hillside to make our ice plant grow,
and rented the monster backhoe

digging out the pool pit to rim it with lava stone
against the mud. My father waved the baton

of his shovel to light the fuse to the chord
of dynamited stone: the cloud of our need

went up all over California
and rang in overtones all through me.

Detectives

The two detectives prowling at the edges of my dream are late—as usual. Already I'm being pushed toward the cliff edge, driven not by a gunman or a maniac, but by wanting to escape my betrayal of a friend—a serious betrayal, worth thirty pieces of silver. On all the talk shows, they talk about how I lie, about my need for attention and how no stunt is too low to get it. But when they tell how I sold out my friend, my dismissal of kindness and decency, like leaving your wife when she has cancer, the shame is too much. Off the cliff I fall, until the ground looms up, and the detectives come running—the man wearing the years-long death mask of detachment, the woman, who's only been dead a few days, the mask of death as disillusion. And in their eyes, there's something so heartbroken, so lonely! As if their work as detectives, almost sacred in their minds, had been made into a sideshow by bad actors on TV, and I was their last chance—muffed again!—to prove to the world what was good and true in being a real detective. And so to make them feel less defeated, I start to lie, denying I betrayed her. . . . And the veiled triumph in the man's eyes at having caught me in my lies look like my father's eyes, so that I know just what he's feeling when he reaches to take his partner's hand—a hand so like my mother's that when she reaches to take mine, I recognize her passionate avowal undercut by wariness, sounding the same as in life: *We'll stand by you,* she says, her cool grasp assuring me that they know I know that all I'm pretending they don't know we all know, but look, that's OK, we're family, aren't we? a family of detectives?

"Let Thanks Be Given to the Raven as Is Its Due"

I read a story, I'd like to think it's true,
about a raven in Rome who lived
above a shoemaker's shop and every day the bird flew

to the Capitol where it greeted the Senators by name:
magnificent sounding names, Germanicus, Drusus,
Decimus Brutus, even Emperor Tiberius just come

from Capri where, for a wrong prediction, he'd thrown
his astrologer off a cliff. The raven
was no snob, though, he greeted the people of Rome

as they passed by, with names like Paulus,
Paulina—the same name as my long-dead great aunt
who lived in Newark in an apartment complex so notorious

for heroin that one day when I visited her
she talked that way . . . that way that makes you wonder
how a woman who was a social worker,

a Eugene Debs Socialist, could become so vicious in
her mind. But the courteous raven spoke
with such virtue that it seemed more than human—

and when the raven greeted Tiberius, who kept everyone
in a creeping state of terror, he called back a greeting,
blessing the bird as a good omen for Rome.

And year in year out, the raven flew
to the Capitol and greeted every morning the soon-
to-be poisoned, the soon-to-be suicides, the thinker who

would open his veins in the bath, the arbiter
of pleasure who knew his days were few
and so to read Sappho meant, in his last hours,

to forget a little of his fear. And the raven
greeted the prostitute who had the contest with Messalina,
great wife of Caesar, and Messalina won:

twenty-five men in twenty-four hours, which might not sound
like all that many, barely more than one an hour,
but it isn't the number, is it? The bird perhaps knew that men

and women are the sole animals whose first experience
of mating makes them regret which is why the bird, caught
between two natures, must have felt the aura of Tiberius,

the need of Messalina, but hailed them anyway—
the way it would have hailed Rome's thieves and slaves
and commoners like my aunt running the gauntlet of junkies

she passed through each day in her apartment complex's hallways,
just teenage kids, some of them, who liked the taste of junk—
though two or three did try to rob her, and the super told me,

when my mother and I finally found a place to move her,
how the kids liked to torment her, shouting out,
"You old white bitch!" which she returned with her slurs—

or think of Tiberius's apparent modesty in refusing
the groveling Senate's honors, the way his outward show
of virtue—he forbade all public kissing—

gave morality a high tone: did his power
at last unmask him? So that he found relief
in training little boys to swim under

and between his legs, little licking, nibbling fishes, while
nursing babies were given his cock to suck and highborn
Roman women he raped he put on trial

if they fought against him so that one stabbed herself
to be free of his lust; or during a religious sacrifice
he was so taken by the acolyte that he rushed him off

and his flute-playing brother too, not even
waiting for the priest to finish, and afterward,
when they complained, he had their legs broken.

And in affairs of state, his cruelty watched
over twenty executions in a day, the bodies dragged
with hooks into the Tiber, and any man whose estate he coveted

could only find relief from his threats by cutting his own throat.
That's one version of Rome the histories tell—
the same as my version of my aunt is certainly not

how she'd tell it. Which makes the raven's shadow
perched above the Capitol an inkblot shape that can turn
into a nightmare, even as its feathers split into rainbows

the spectra of the sun. Flying home one day, the raven shit
from the air and soiled the shoes of the shoemaker
next door, and the man killed the bird, the records don't

say how, whether with a stone or poison
or a net or strangled or crushed by the man's hands.
The people of Rome flocked to the man's home,

they drove him from the neighborhood,
they lynched him—while the bird's funeral was celebrated
with pomp: a black-draped bier was carried

on sturdy shoulders of two Ethiopians as a flute-player led
them past masses of funeral flowers heaped up
on the way to the pyre built on the right-hand side

of the great Appian Road at the second milestone, on what has
the unlikely name the Rediculus Plain spelled not
with an "i" but an "e"—after the Roman god Rediculus,

deity of returning travelers and of opening and closing
doors, who shut the door on the raven's tomb. And just as the door
was sealed, the risen ghost of Christ came passing by and, meeting

at the bird's pyre his disciple Peter
who would soon be asking to be nailed to his own cross
upside down so as not to compete with his master,

told Peter that He, the Son of Man,
King of the Jews, was a dark bird of omen
returning to Rome to be crucified a second time.

The Animals in the Zoo Don't Seem Worried

"If a lion could talk, we could not understand him."
— *Wittgenstein,* Philosophical Investigations

Looking at the lion behind the plate glass,
I wasn't sure what I was looking at: a lion, OK,
but he seemed to come apart, not literally

I mean, but I couldn't see him whole:
Mane. Teeth. The slung belly pumping
as he panted and began to roar. His balls

sheathed in fur swaying a little. His tail's tuft
jerking in an arc like an old-time pump handle
rusted in mid-air. Somebody or something

I read once said that when Jesus had his vision
of what his father, God, would do to him,
that Jesus could only see pieces of a cross,

pieces of a body appearing through flashes
of sun, as if the body in his vision
was hands looking for feet, a head for a torso,

everything come unmagnetized from the soul:
the lion caught me in his stare not at
or through me but fixated on the great chain

of being that Jesus couldn't see and that
a zebra might gallop in—black and white stripes
marking longitudes of this world turning

to meat, bloody meat—this vision of an inmate
that Jesus's father helped to orchestrate by
making a cageless cage with glass instead

of bars—though the lion didn't seem to care,
he was roaring for his keepers to bring
him food, so everything's what it should be

if you're a lion. Nor did the sea lion
seem concerned about having gone a little
crazy, barking incessantly so I could see

the plush, hot pink insides of its throat,
though like the lion through the glass
there's this distortion, my reflection

I'm looking through that makes me float above
the zoo: and now this silence at closing time
pours like a waterfall in different zones

of silences that, pouring through my head,
surround roaring, barking, human muttering—
is any of that what being sounds like?

Or is it just animal gasping like what
Jesus must have heard from the thieves
hanging beside him, one damned, one saved?

What was in his heart when his vision
clarified and he saw it was a hand he
recognized that the nail was driving through?

The Twins

You know those twins hanging on the corner,
      they look like me and my twin brother
when we were younger, in our twenties,
      the paler one like me, sickly, more uptight,
but weirdly aristocratic, more distant
      than the one like you, Tim, who, if
you were him would put his arm around me
      with that casualness and gentleness
I've always craved between us, which we
      nearly lost in our twenties but got back
in our fifties now that death's in my face
      when I look at it at just the right angle:
then your smile's so open, Tim, that we go
      back even further, to when we were
boys listening on the stairs to our older
      brother telling us about girls, what
you could do with them, what they'd do
      with you . . . not much like our board games
when all we'd think about was rolling
      the dice and moving the metal dog or battleship
round and round the squares, counting out loud,
      intent on winning . . . but these past few days
your eyes keep confronting me in the mirror,
      your glance full of a goofball happiness!
And the wreath of poppies around your head
      grazes my forehead too, and like the dope
I used to shoot, the clear dose in the syringe
      lets me down into my body like I'm deep
inside your body, the two of us together
      fed by the same blood, waking, sleeping,

nestled next to each other, thumbs in our mouths—
         but it only lasts a little while, this feeling
of me inside you inside that liquid warmth
         up the back of my neck and down toward
my cock, the high moving at its own sweet will—
         Tim, I'll only belong to you forever
when the other brother, the pale and stern
         and faceless one who holds the needle still
when I slide it into the vein and smiles back
         my smile, I'll only belong to him too when he,
in some parody of an old rocker in a crowd
         of old rockers holding up lit cigarette lighters,
snaps shut that flickering: oh sure,
         to sleep is good, to die is even better,
but the best is never to have been born.

2

Homage to Zidane

In all the cafés
on the seafront
whatever could be seen
kept exploding in riots

of blue, red, green—
horns everywhere hooting
for the ball soaring
toward the net.

Slicks of trash
and plastic glinting
from the waves, the world
was in a fever

to see the perfect goal,
the giant screens
on every corner
loud with the locust thrum

of satellite hookups.
Between two limestone cliffs
I plunged into the filth,
sucked a mouthful

of oil
and set out
swimming hard
to where I heard

rising voices
shouting in Arabic
Score Score.
A big wave swept

me under,
another and another,
until I shot out
of the water that gleamed

like a forehead butting mine,
expert but without malice
threatening to drag me down
until I slid out on the rocks.

I shivered, and wanted to live
in the clear light
of the announcers' voices
echoing in different languages

weaving a net so fine
the sun could pass through it—
yet you could see
in instant replay

the ball caught and caught
and caught, and not one stitch
of that fabric
going taut.

Refugee Camp

When one of the soldiers asked me about my fever,
despite the fact that I was almost seeing double,
and I couldn't get my head clear of the zebra
I'd seen killed by lions the day before—
$\qquad\qquad\qquad\qquad\qquad$ the zebra
on its side, striped legs jerking, twitching, as their heads
disappeared, necks shoved up to the shoulders
into its belly—
$\qquad\qquad\qquad$ I said, *No, the fever's better,*
let's go for a ride.
$\qquad\qquad\qquad\qquad$ So he put me on the back
of his motorbike, an ancient Honda 160
with blown-out baffles so it made a rackety,
popping roar that split my head in two.
The old Somali poet, as we took off, was still reciting
his poem about wanting to go home:
$\qquad\qquad\qquad\qquad\qquad\qquad$ beard stiff
with henna, his old pants immaculately clean
despite the dust and living in a hut with a floor
made of flattened out CARE cardboard
from unpacked medical supplies.

The United States must help us, he sang,
and, *What do you have for me, now that I have taken time*
from my busy schedule to sing for you?
I had nothing to give him and so I smiled
a sort of hangdog smile—which was when the soldier said:
How is your fever? Would you like to go for a ride?

Dust and wind and engine-throb blacked out
any sound so we were completely cocooned
in our own cloud, muffling grayness spreading
ear to ear—
                         my arms wrapped around the soldier's waist,
his sweating shirtback drying into my sweating shirtfront,
we passed the compound where an hour ago
I heard a woman tell the registration officer,
nervously giggling through the translator's English,
that she'd been "done to"—
                                              a young woman with large eyes,
solidly built, holding a cell phone she kept
looking down at as if expecting it to ring—
while other women at other desks stared into
digital cameras taking their photos,
biometric scans of face and fingerprints,
fingerprints then inked the old-fashioned way
into a dossier, questions and answers,
any known enemies, was your husband
or brother part of a militia, which militia?
Faces looking back from computer screens
logging each face into the files, 500 each day
lining up outside the fences, more and more
wanting in as the soldier and the motorbike's
grit and oil-fume haze stinging my skin
cast a giant shadow-rider riding alongside us,
human and machine making a new being
not even a hyena, who eats everything,
even the bones, could hold in its jaws.

Nostrils parching, the gouged road drifted deep
made my fever rear back as the bike
hit a rise and fishtailed, almost crashing
into a pothole while I hung on
tighter, not in the least bit scared, as if all my fever
could take in was what the single-cylinder
two-stroke piston inside its housing kept on
shouting, *Now that you have come here,
do you like what you see? Is this your first time?
Are you hungry? Thirsty? Tired? Sad? Sick? Happy?*

Hunger

In places where I am and he isn't,
in places where he is and I'm not, if
he's survived, if his baby teeth have grown

past rudiments of mouthing, now he bites
and chews, his will driven by craving for what
might be there and might not in the food sacks

that if you put your head in them smell not
at all, as if the grain weren't real, or made
of molecules extraterrestrial, a substance

never seen on earth before, a substance
that in the huge warehouse rises in
a pyramid, grain sacks stacked into

a mock Pharaoh's tomb so if a human-headed
bird with an infant's face should fly up
in green-winged splendor sprouting from bony

shoulderblades and feathering his neck
muscles so exhausted they minutely
tremble, unable to hold his head

upright for more than a few seconds, wouldn't it
be hard, almost impossible, for his winged *Ba*
to dissolve into *Akh* where his molecules bend

into beams of light?—and so he stays in *Duat,*
nothing transfigured, as in this moment:
to get a better look at me, steel turtle head

in flak jacket, he cocks his head almost
like a bird's, his sidelong famine gawk,
as he lies listless in his mother's lap,

coming back into focus when the woman
from *Médecins Sans Frontières* gives him
Plumpy'Nut that needs no water, no refrigeration,

no preparation, a food suited to eternity,
so that body, becoming *Ba,* may eat to enter *Akh,*
unless you're shut out, unless you live

forever in your death in *Duat,* condemned
forever to eat this peanut slurry as a biscuit
that he chews and chews . . . but when he's finished

he begins throwing the silver wrapper
in the air, catching it and throwing it
fluttering in the air, the silver wrapper

turning the air between him and his mother
into a medium, another otherworld
nobody but them can share just as long

as the calories, the sugars, the digestive
juices feed that silver-never-ending-
in-the-moment-momentary fluttering.

Eclipse
for Tayeb Salih and Binyavanga Wainaina

Heat lightning flicking between head and heart
and throat makes me hesitate: I could see
in the rearview one part of the story
while up ahead the crowd breaking into riot

were throwing rocks at one another as the soldiers
retreated into a doorway. The whole thing
comes back like a moment out of Eisenstein,
the baby carriage bumping fast and faster

down the city stairs, screaming mouths ajar—
and that's when I smelled an overripe lily smell,
an eye-corroding battery-acid smell:

tear gas in a green cloud came wafting
from the mosque, all of us imploding
into the eyes staring from next day's newspaper.

꩜

"Oh yahhh, we got plenty of carjackers here, Mr. Tom.
Two fellows, I see them in the rearview mirror, one
with a *panga,* the other with a gun,
and so I put the car in reverse and drove right over them.

But you journalists are crazy, you like all this—
after the elections when we Kikuyus
were being hunted down at all the checkpoints
the fellows I was driving for, good guys sure, they want

to find the worst thing and shoot it for TV.
And so they stop the car near a stack of burning tires
and inside the tires is a Kikuyu like me

and they tell me I'm safe, we don't have to worry
because we're the press: but that damned fine fellow in the fire,
if he was me, would I just be part of the story?"

～

Later, in a *matatu* blaring "Sexual Healing," I sat
staring at a poster of a punk rocker without
her shirt on, two machine pistols
held at just the right angles to hide her nipples.

It made me weirdly happy to look at her—
her, and the light coming through the windows,
and the jerk of the *matutu* through giant potholes,
and the lifting off of whatever fear

into the logic of a dream where I was some new life form
sent down for no larger purpose
than to listen to the talk-show host ask questions

about "the alpha female," "foreign influences"
that make riots happen,
and if "the President is going to plant some trees."

～

When she wrote about Africa, note that "People"
means Africans who aren't black while "The People"
means Africans who are. She never mentions AK-47s
(which don't yet exist), but prominent ribs, naked breasts. Lions

she always treats as well-rounded characters
with public school accents while hyenas
come off vaguely Middle Eastern. Bad characters
include children of Tory cabinet ministers, Afrikaners,

and future employees of the World Bank.
She always takes the side of elephants, no matter who they trample.
This is before "blood diamonds" or nightclubs called Tropicana

where mercenaries, prostitutes, expats, and nouveau-riche Africans
    hang out.
But there were genitals, mutilated genitals.
And of course her *sotto* voice, her sad *I-expected-so-much* tone.

                   ✍

A nail in the wall is what the world hangs on:
a poster of the latest "big man" whose name
in fifty years nobody will know; or Jesus looking
put upon, head drooping on the cross, hands bleeding

a hundred times over in the wooden gallery
of tiny Jesuses for sale. Or else a mosquito net
drapes down in a gauzy canopy
over the narrow, self-denying cot

where you sleep for a few hours, sweating out
malaria between parsing words
writing the fatal formula that cuts

into the mind terms you can't live with or without:
"We are foreign men in a white world,
or foreign-educated men in a black world."

The plate glass shattering rewound into the windows,
cannisters of tear gas leapt back into the hands that threw them,
even the horns hooting and the awful traffic jam
reversed into dawn and malarial mosquitoes

drifting in my room. The power hadn't come back on,
the air was completely still, and overhead the sun
passed behind the moon—everything in motion
uneasy as clouds shifting. I imagined on

the road the sound of different footsteps,
slap of sandals, leather soles' soft creak, the sun
dissolving in its own corona in its arc

across the continent to blaze out above ships
plowing through the Indian Ocean while millions
of shoes on the tarmac walk and walk to work.

KM4

1/ THE MOUTH

Not English Somali Italian French the mouth
blown open in the Toyota battle wagon at KM4
speaks in a language never heard before.

Not the Absolute Speaker of the News,
not crisis chatter's famine/flame,
the mouth blown open at KM4
speaks in a language never heard before.

Speaks back to the dead at KM4,
old men in *macawis,* beards dyed with henna,
the women wearing blue jeans under black *chadors.*

Nothing solved or resolved, exactly as they were,
the old wars still flickering in the auras round their faces,
the mouth of smoke at KM4
mouths syllables of smoke never heard before.

2/ THE CONCERT

Lake water
in smooth still sun moves in
and out of synch
with the violin
playing at the villa—

the bow attacking the strings looks like a hand
making some frantic motion to come closer, go away—

it's hard to say what's being said,
who's being summoned from the dead,
from red sand drifting
across the sheen of the shining floor.

The pianist's hands taking wing to hover above a chord
become the flight path
of a marabou stork crashing down
on carrion, the piano levitating up and up
above red sand that it starts to float across

the way a camel's humps
far off in the mirage rise and fall fall and rise
until mirage overbrims itself
and everything into its shimmering disappears.

And the ones who died the day before,
blown up at the crossroads at KM4,
scanning the notice board for scholarship results,
put their fingers to their names as the onlookers applaud.

3/ ORACLE

The little man carved out of bone
shouts something to the world the world can't hear.
All around him the roads, lost in drifted, deep red sand,
die out in sun just clearing the plain.

Dried out, faded, he makes an invocation at an altar:
an AK-47 stood up on its butt end in a pile of rock.

The AK talks the talk of what guns talk—

not rage or death or clichés of killing,
but specs of what it means to be fired off in the air.

No fear when it jams, no enemy running away,
no feeling like a river overflowing in a cloudburst—

forget all that: the little man of bone is not the streaming head
of the rivergod roaring at Achilles; nor dead Patroclos
complaining in a dream how Achilles has forgotten him.

The AK wants to tell a different truth—
a truth ungarbled that is so obvious
no one could possibly mistake its meaning.

If you look down the cyclops-eye of the barrel
what you'll see is a boy with trousers
rolled above his ankles.

You'll see a mouth of bone moving in syllables
that have the rapid-fire clarity
of a weapon that can fire 600 rounds a minute.

4/ "BEFORE HE BLEW HIMSELF UP, HE LIKED
TO PLAY AT GAMES WITH OTHER YOUTHS."

And there, among the dead, appearing beside your tent flap,
at your elbow in the mess hall,
waiting to use, or just leaving, the showers and latrine,
the boy with his trousers rolled appears
like an afterimage burned into an antique computer screen,
haunting whatever the cursor tries to track.

So he liked to play at games with other youths?

The English has the slightly
too-formal sound of someone
being poured through the sieve of another language.

Syllable after syllable
piling up and up until the boy,
buried to the neck,
slowly vanishes into overtones that are and are not his.

As if he were a solid melting to liquid turning to gas feeding a flame.

5/ TIME TO FORGET

There's a camel a goat a sandal left in red sand.

Over there's a water tower, under that's the bore hole
and here the body asks and asks about the role
it's asked to play: no matter how it's dressed.

Like a nomad like a journalist like the hyena
who eats even the bones
and shits bone-white scat from the calcium.

No matter if it sleeps under a dome
of UNHCR plastic, baby blue in the sun,
or hides in a spider hole
or walks around in uniform behind plate glass,
the body makes itself known before it becomes unknown.

On the television the blade runner is facing down the skinjob,
and of the two, who is the more human?
On the table there isn't a glass of whiskey but the ghost of whiskey
that keeps whispering, *It's OK to be this way, nobody will know.*

And then the boy who rolls his pantlegs
up above his ankles because to let them drag along the ground
is to be unclean turns right before your eyes into a skeleton.

6/ THE COMING

At KM4 a wall of leaves spits green into the air
and hangs there beautiful and repulsive.

Between the leaves, in the interstices where birds
don't stir in sun and heat, the smell of raw camel meat
wakes you to the vision of what keeps going on in the wound—

the wound inside your head that you more or less shut out
as you go round and round the roundabout
at KM4 where your friends the soldiers in the Casspir
are all pretending to be dead.

The TV Ken doll anchor keeps complaining to their corpses,
*Hey, can't you get my flak jacket adjusted
so it doesn't crush my collar?*

Leaves softly undulating, little waves of leaves undergoing shifts
between astral blue and green, leaves always breaking on leaves
in the little breeze that the Casspir passing stirs in the heat—

stirring the memory of putting your fingers
in the wounds of a blast wall at KM4 as if you were
doubting Thomas waiting for Christ to appear:

thumb-sized holes for AK-47s,
fist-sized for twenty caliber, both fists for fifty.

7/ RAP

Out of a mouth of bone that lives inside
the darkness in a stone like a cricket hidden
somewhere inside a dark house, the incessant stridulation
sounds like the song, *I would love to be martyred in
Allah's Cause and then get resurrected
and then get martyred and then get resurrected
again and then get martyred . . .*

If your trouser legs drag on
the ground you're sullied, you're unclean.
Be a Fedayeen. Be a Marine. On the other side
of language where none of the concepts stick
the boy with his trousers rolled liked
what he called "the rap music"
and a t-shirt emblazoned with the word "Knicks."

8/ AT COURT

Off behind the acacias in a little oasis of galvanized shade
the soldiers sit smoking and joking,
they talk to you with shy smiles and gentle laughter,
they offer cigarettes before you can offer them,
their tact and manners are exquisite.

It's like being at a king's court where the thrones
are three-legged stools, where the knights before battle
go around in regulation-issue sleeveless undershirts,
where the gold and silver floor is dust packed hard by boots.

Now the wind is blowing through the trees,
the scene is changing as the day moon grows strong,
leaves hanging from the branches
drip and curdle in the afternoon sun.

The soldiers lie down on mats, their faces slacken,
sleep runs like a hand over their skinny bodies,
and a goat climbs into a huge cooking pot
and licks and licks the sides clean.

9/ REUNION

The journalist who doesn't sleep walks into a bullet.

The young boy with trousers rolled waits at KM4.

Before them both is a door into the earth that swings back
like a cellar door in the last century.

Ahmed Abdi Ali Patrice Andy Bill Rika Zero Idil Yoko
meet in the underworld at The Greasepit Bar
and talk about rotations up to the world of the living:

they come back like Patroclos to accuse dreaming Achilles
of having forgotten and forsaken him,
faithless in death to their companions . . .

The sun compressed to a sliver shines through
mesh of my mosquito net that holds back
mosquitos hovering like the souls I don't believe in
of those who've died or have gone missing in the wind's
unsubtle devastatations—

but the love of lost companions
brings back wet underwear: socks, T-shirts,
boxer shorts, bras, panties, a dhoti
hung from thorn trees to dry in the dawn breeze.

10/ TOO LATE

Here the body is the sheered-off wing of the Trans-Avia plane
lying in a scrapheap
like the knocked-off arm of an old Grecian figurine
of Winged Victory pacing down the deck of Athenian might.

Here, you can let yourself go in so many ways—
the bomb pack strapped to your waist and detonated
by pushing Send on your cell phone.

Or the eternal aesthete in his eternal pursuit
of just the right moment to see
the splintering of light passing through tent mesh
waking you to the unambivalent hate you've always craved.

The rivals walk off to where the broken pediments
of the cathedral still brace under the weight of the rose window.

And the body barters for the ghosts pinned down by the shadows
to come rising at this moment from the grave
telling the body it's too late, it's always been too late
passing over the ocean's dry whispering wave.

3

Homage to Bashō
for Christopher Merrill

WHAT I HAVE TO SAY ABOUT MY TRIP MEANDERS the way the Tigris and Euphrates meander, and like those rivers in flood, is sometimes murky in intention, balked in it its conclusions, and flows where it has to flow. In Iraq, in which the customs and conventions were often operating invisibly, or easily misinterpreted to be the same as mine, I suppose I gave up on telling a straightforward story. Instead, one night in a helicopter, what I felt in the air, so different from what was happening on the ground, made me realize that when you take an oath to tell the truth, you're not telling that truth either to the judge or to the courtroom. Perhaps the point of the oath is to try to surround yourself with a lightness and solitude from which you can speak the truth, adding whatever light and shade you can so as to make "the how" implicate "the why." After all, the judge and the members of the court weren't riding in the helicopter, so a realistic description won't mean anything to anyone unless you add that light and shade which only you, as the witness, could perceive.

But even then, in the helicopter roar, the truth may be hard to hear, even in your own ears.

VILLANELLE ON GOING TO BAGHDAD

Again and again I kept taking a picture of the numbers
and letters on my passport for Deneyse from Texas,
just the same as me, except she was in Baghdad and I was where

I was feeling ridiculous, a real techno-fumbler,
as I downloaded and uploaded and pressed
Send over and over, trying to get the numbers

and letters to come out right: 2211 . . . and then a lot of blur
that was driving Deneyse crazy: *Who is this jackass
that he can't even use a cell phone?* She was stuck where

she was stuck, in the desert in the Green Zone, and here
I was, listening to some unknown bird doing its best
to sound like a wind-up bird while the numbers

and letters got screwed up in the electronic ether—
my cell phone's camera kept making my passport face
explode with little yellow stars, and I didn't know where

in what universe they came from, my face like the numbers
and letters and that screeching bird devolving to this creeping
    sense
of senselessness making me vestigially aware of how numbers

and letters and maybe Deneyse too, despite whatever
she was trained to show as her Embassy face,
were all part of this giant abstraction branching out everywhere

just like a tree that every second keeps getting bigger
until it dwarfed me and her and the bird, dwarfed
the embassy, and my silly attempts to make the numbers

and letters more readable: and then I was aware
of my heart, I mean my real heart, the bloody muscle inside my
    chest,
beating a little too fast, telling me in a melodramatic way, *Beware

the Ides of March!* like the soothsayer in *Julius Caesar.*
And then no bird, no embassy, no Deneyse,
no me—there were just the pictures of letters and numbers
hanging from the tree and Baghdad was a nowhere anywhere.

I FLEW SOUTH TO BASRA IN A DASH 8, an eager little commuter plane with a fifty-seat capacity. The loadmaster—which is Embassy Air speak for the steward—wore wraparounds and a reflective orange and yellow caution vest. "File across the airstrip single file," he told us. "Avoid the propellers, and climb the stairs into the Dash one pair of feet on the stairs at a time." The only addition to the safety announcement was the loadmaster warning us that the plane might shoot off decoy flares, and that the explosion we would hear was the sound of the flares deploying. If a heat-seeking, infra-red guided missile was fired at the Dash, automatic sensors would release the flares, either in clusters or one by one, in the hope that the flare's heat signature, many times hotter than the engine, would decoy the IR missile away from us and after the flare. On an earlier flight to Baghdad, Chris, my pal and fellow traveler, had experienced the release of these flares: "The explosion," he said, "was really loud, loud enough to hurt your ears, and absolutely terrifying."

The plane began to taxi down the runway, and Chris and I fell silent as the rattle and roar of the Dash ascending filled the cabin.

GOING TO BASRA

Shamash the sun god, the god of justice who lays bare
the righteous and the wicked when he floods the world
with light, came walking down
the muddy-looking Tigris
into Basra where gas flares from the refineries burning all night
    long
faded into the Dash 8's prop
whirring just beyond the window.

So much gas was burning off into the air the plane
was descending through
that a skin of light kept rippling over the city's cinderblock and
    rebar
tilting up at the plane's belly swooping down.

In my book I read how the Deluge made the dykes give way:
the gods crouch like dogs with their tails between their legs,
terrified at the storm-demons they themselves let loose.
At the end of six days and nights, Utnapishtim and his wife
send out a raven that never returns.
The ark runs aground on a mountaintop just above the storm
    waters
that have beaten the world flat into mud and clay.

And Utnapishtim and his wife offer the gods sweet cane, myrtle,
    cedar,
and the gods smell the savor,
the gods smell the sweet savor,
the gods hover like flies over the sweetness.

THE PLANE LEVELED OFF AT CRUISING ALTITUDE, and through the pit-
ted glass, I saw the Tigris winding through Baghdad, the city hazy in
the morning light. As we flew south, the Euphrates and Tigris, which
almost meet in Baghdad, again diverged into widely meandering beds
before coming together outside of Basra in a river called the Shatt al-
Arab that empties into the Persian Gulf. Field on field of green wheat
and barley surrounded small isolated farmsteads nestled inside groves
of date palms. Underneath us, I watched the shadow of the Dash ripple
across the vast green plain between the Tigris and Euphrates. Mes-
opotamia means "the land between the rivers," and here and there,
you could see long, straight irrigation canals, and artificial reservoirs
divided up by dykes, watering the fields. I was astonished to actually

be seeing what I had known since grade school as "the cradle of civilization." I remember reading about cuneiform writing, and thinking that it looked like the marks that a flock of crows' feet would leave in our muddy garden if it froze solid overnight.

As we began to see the outskirts of Basra, I thought of the great Ziggurat at Ur, and how, twenty-five years ago—and a year or so before the first Gulf War broke out—I'd come across a cuneiform tablet in the Louvre, translated into French, about the destruction of Ur. I copied it out on the back of an envelope, took it home, where it sat on my desk for months while I read the odes of Horace. And then one day, I found it on my desk, and thought that if I could treat it like an Horatian ode, that I might be able to do something with it in English. So via a French translation of an ancient Akkadian original, and utilizing a meter that I'd come across in Horace, I translated a poem into English that I called "Lamentation on Ur." I hadn't meant the poem to have overt political overtones—I thought of it as a general comment on the destruction and fragility of civilized life:

LAMENTATION ON UR
    —*from a Sumerian spell, 2000 BC*

Like molten bronze and iron shed blood
        pools. Our country's dead
melt into the earth
        as grease melts in the sun, men whose
helmets now lie scattered, men annihilated

by the double-bladed axe. Heavy, beyond
        help, they lie still as a gazelle
exhausted in a trap,
        muzzle in the dust. In home
after home, empty doorways frame the absence

of mothers and fathers who vanished
        in the flames remorselessly
spreading claiming even
        frightened children who lay quiet
in their mother's arms, now borne into

oblivion, like swimmers swept out to sea
        by the surging current.
May the great barred gate
        of blackest night again swing shut
on silent hinges. Destroyed in its turn,

may this disaster too be torn out of mind.

BUT THEN THE GULF WAR CAME ALONG, and suddenly the poem was taken up as an anti-war poem: so current events had transformed what I thought of as a general statement into a topical, political statement. And soon I would be flying just to the west of the Great Ziggurat, damaged by 400 bullet holes and five large bomb craters made by US warplanes as they bombed a nearby Iraqi airbase.

I remember teaching a class of undergraduates in which a young Iraqi woman, who had lived through the bombardments of Desert Storm, sat among us. The students had no idea that she was from Iraq, nor did I, until she wrote a paper about surviving the bombing. I asked her before class if I could use her paper as part of the discussion, and whether she would mind talking about the bombardment that she had lived through. She agreed, a slight girl wearing a beige head scarf, with perfectly plucked, and absolutely symmetrical eyebrows. She was a very soft-spoken young woman, and her command of English was perfect, though more formal than the English most of the students spoke.

We were reading the *Iliad,* and were talking about the anatomical particularity with which Homer describes the wounding and death of the individual heroes. I asked them to think about the only war that they knew at that time, the first Gulf War, and to discuss their sense of whether or not, given the images of backs and lungs and livers and bellies pierced through by spearheads, it was possible to justify the slaughter of war, including the civilians killed as "collateral damage." Almost the entire class, women as well as men, said that it was possible to justify the slaughter, based on American interests abroad, on overcoming dictators for democracy, and on the hope that a better life could come out of battle. I then asked them what they would say to someone who had actually lived through the bombardments to achieve these worthy goals—and that this someone was here, sitting among them, as one of their fellow classmates? How would they explain to their classmate the necessity of the bombs? Silence fell on the room. Everyone looked deeply uncomfortable: I realized that I'd betrayed them, as well as the young Iraqi woman, who sat very still in her seat, though I hadn't meant to. I'd assumed that there would be at least some opposition to the "just war" thesis, and I was disconcerted when I realized that not one of them had moral qualms, or at least qualms that they were willing to express. And then one boy said, "I guess if I were that person, I'd think that most of what I just said was pretty stupid." And when I asked the young woman to talk about her experience, she said something like: "We sat in our house with the lights off. The bombs went on for a long time, and when they stopped, all of us were so tired, we went to sleep." She plucked her head scarf a little further over her hair, fell silent—and then the class ended.

ZIGGURAT

What's built collapses
to be rebuilt, ruin on top
of ruin piling up into
a ziggurat pocked by shell holes

so that our knowledge is the knowledge
of drifting sand, grit in the cupboard,
grit under the bed where a doll's head,
button eyes open, lies forgotten.

We will be covered by the dune
and uncovered in time,
our helmet straps wasted away,
metal eaten through—

though we, the fallen, perpetually
on guard, will stare back at you
from the streaked bathroom mirror,
making yourselves presentable to the light of day.

For us, the marshlands drained and turned
to dust will be our present kingdom,
our spectral waterway among the always instant reeds,
shivering, bending to the current.

﹏

I PROVED MYSELF TO BE INEPT at putting on my bulletproof vest,
attaching this to that in all the wrong places, before figuring out how
to velcro the waist panels tightly around my stomach so that they were
under the vest, not over it, and adjusting and readjusting the shoulder
straps to make sure they were tight. I didn't look very military: in fact,
I looked like I was wearing a bib, a sort of Rambo, Jr.

Now that I was strapped into my vest, it felt fairly light weight,
around eight pounds—thick enough, according to the specs, to give
reasonable protection against handguns. But when you consider that
a bullet fired from a military-style weapon is the equivalent of a five-
pound sledgehammer smashing into you at forty-five miles per hour,
serious bruising and broken ribs are pretty much guaranteed. I put on

my helmet and snapped the chin-snap fast, but I had to keep pushing it back from sliding down over my eyes. Rather than protected, I looked—and felt—like an overgrown infant.

In front of our armored vehicle—a Chevy Suburban SUV reinforced with steel plating—a beefy, but terminally polite security contractor dressed in khakis, a brown knit shirt, a gray windbreaker, lightweight hikers, and sporting a buzz-cut, gave us a briefing: "Once you're inside the vehicle, please stay away from the doors. We'll let you in and out. If we take fire, or if I give you the signal to get down, I'd appreciate it if you could get on the bottom of the vehicle. I'll climb in back with you and cover you. Once we get to our destination, you can leave your armor and helmets in the vehicle. Then we'll open the doors, and we'll proceed single file to our destination. Everything clear?"

CAR COVER

The car cover blown halfway off the car
billows and bags, sagging back
to a slack void before being blown wide
open, almost as if a man, or a man and woman,
or a woman and her soldier
wrestled over and over, amorous
and/or murderous
in the cold Brooklyn wind, the weak Christmas Day sun
lighting in stark shadow the shredded
plastic bags billowing in leafless branches
above what keeps billowing
below, a duet singing what's above
to what's below, sky and earth concentrating
all their powers on what could be three, or four,
or countless small wars
rolling over the earth's surface
the way the canvas rolls in the animating wind,

the corners at war with the center
they want to tear free of, the center
tugging and yanking at the corners—
but it's all just a piece of canvas sewn
to fit over roof and windshield and hug bumper
and headlights, so ingeniously
tailored that even this small skill rebukes me
for my seeing in its roiling
sullen gas flares
breaking out all over the earth, and the security contractors
who are paid to keep me safe
wearing their in-ear radio receivers
hearing what's going on out there as we move
in the armored Suburban among the lucky and the doomed
until one or the other or both
lie still as the car cover
going slack over the skin of the abandoned car.

༺

IN ONE OF OUR WORKSHOPS, a slight young woman wearing a black and white headscarf, with a round face and large black eyes, and with just a hint of mascara on the lashes, stood up to read her poem. Her name, I think, was Mariam, and she stood very straight in front of her classmates, and read to us with a quiet, unself-conscious dignity. Her pronunciation was excellent so I have a good memory of what she wrote. She said that she was woken near dawn by her older brother in her bedroom, who had bent down to gently kiss her on the cheek, and to ask her if she wanted anything special in the market. And when she looked up at him, to tell him "No," he said to her, very gently, that this would be the last time she'd be seeing him. But she was so sleepy, she didn't quite take in what he meant, and a moment later he was gone. Later that morning, she wrote, she was in the kitchen having breakfast with her mother. And then their neighbor came in and gave them the news. She wrote that as she heard the news, she felt herself get smaller and disappear: she had no hands, no face, no body to feel with. There was no kitchen, no mother, no her. The neighbor, she wrote, told them about the "car accident." She wrote how she remembers her brother's words coming back to her, how gentle he was when he kissed her on the cheek, how he would always bring her special things from the market. And then she sat down, seeming completely self-possessed, except for the sadness that had come into her voice and hung now in the room. No one said anything for a while, as what she hadn't said—didn't need to say, since everyone in her generation already understood—resonated for a few moments. Chris and I looked at each other, but were slower in grasping what it was she'd left out. And then it dawned on us too: her brother had been a suicide bomber and blown himself up in the car.

～

FOR ALL THE VIOLENCE GOING ON IN IRAQ, in my little white box of a CHU, my container housing unit, it was eerily calm. And no wonder: the entire complex of CHUs was covered by a huge steel roof and surrounded by twenty-foot high, reinforced concrete blast walls—"to keep bombs and missiles from falling right on your head" was how the fellow who gave me the key to my CHU put it. This kept the whole compound perpetually in shadow, but it added to the feeling of isolation and quiet.

There's a poem by Tomas Tranströmer in which he's in a motel room so anonymous that faces of his old patients begin to push through the walls. The CHU was something like that, a refuge from the violence, a deprivation chamber I was grateful to retreat to, but also a little theater of the mind in which what happened during the day came back to haunt me in the ammonia smell of disinfectant mixed with drying mud that exuded from my CHU. Mariam's face came back many times, and the face of her brother, though I could never quite make out his face because it was always too close to hers. I could see the shape of his head as he bent down to her ear, but his body was lost in shadow. His gentleness and the violence of his final act resisted my attempts to explain or understand. Of course, I was imposing on his entire past the moment when he'd pressed Send, making that moment more significant than a thousand other moments which, as he lived them, would have had their own weight and value. A back-page newspaper photo of smoke pouring up, a vague ghost-face pushing forward into the white walls of my CHU—except for the glimpse Mariam had given me, that was all I could see.

Meanwhile, inside my CHU, I led a radically simplified life: no decorations, purely functional furniture, and not much of it—and a gas mask against Sarin and other forms of nerve gas, packed neatly in a small cardboard box with a convenient black plastic handle. The warning read DO NOT REMOVE.

But after a while, staring up at the white ceiling, letting my thoughts drift, I'd remember the daily body count—the bodies, which had seemed so abstract back in the US, began to take on solidity and form. From the very first night in my CHU, I'd established a routine (maybe more of an obsession) of going online to check on that day's violence. During the night and day it took me to reach Iraq, twelve liquor stores, run mainly by Yazidi Kurds, had been shot up in drive-bys from SUVs: nine customers and owners had been killed. Although no official group stepped forward, conservative Shia, whose version of Islam decrees death for drinking booze, were probably the gunmen. Then on Sunday, forty-six more people were killed, this time by Sunnis terrorizing mainly Shia neighborhoods: the places they hit were crowded shopping areas, markets, and auto-repair shops. If the bombs had gone off in corresponding borough neighborhoods, they would have been the Fulton Mall in Brooklyn, Hunts Point Market in Queens, and the lower reaches of Fourth Avenue's garages in Gowanus.

～

LATE ONE NIGHT WHEN I COULDN'T SLEEP, I went onto Donald Rumsfeld's website, and clicked onto a secret, now declassified, memo that he had written in 2002, a year before the war began, when he was still Secretary of Defense. It was entitled, appropriately enough, "The

Parade of Horribles." The term derives from the nineteenth-century custom of mummers parades, in which one's fellow townsfolk would dress up like monsters and grotesques, and lurch down Main Street on the 4th of July. I clicked on the memo, and watched as twenty-nine Horribles marched down my screen—including number 13, in which no weapons of mass destruction are discovered. (Rumsfeld himself placed three check marks after this Horrible). Other Horribles include sectarian battles between Sunni, Shia, and Kurds (one check mark); US postwar involvement lasting ten years, not two to four (one check mark); the cost of the war becoming ruinously high (no check mark, though the cost to the United States and Iraq is $200 billion and climbing); and world opinion turning against the US because Iraq would "best us in public relations and persuade the world the war is against Muslims" (five check marks).

DEPOSITION
   after the "Supplemental Report on September 11 Detainees'
   Allegations of Abuse at the Metropolitan Detention Center in
   Brooklyn, New York"

According to Lieutenant 1, he confronted
another lieutenant who was responsible
for escorting detainees (hereinafter "Lieutenant 2")
after seeing Lieutenant 2 slamming detainees against
the wall. Lieutenant 2 also supervised many of the other officers
whom Lieutenant 1 witnessed slam detainees against the wall.

Lieutenant 1 stated that Lieutenant 2
told him that slamming, bouncing, pressing against the wall
were all part of being in jail and not to worry about it. To confront
such things when nations everywhere are responsible
for "Admax"—administrative maximum security—against
terrorist cells puts security staff, particularly frontline officers,

under seismic pressures that make officers confront
not only the many hidden drives that are responsible
for terrorism, but the subtle way the wall,
if detainees breathe or move at all, calls out: whoever is against
terrorism haunts the detainees' minds with the specter of
        Lieutenant 2,
who becomes in the detainees' self-hatred of their own inner officers

a general hatred that rears up into a wall
walling detainees in, nobody now "against"
but all submitting to a kind of law that makes detainees confront
what they would like to see as an officer's pathology, an officer's
need to feel the "Admax" of being responsible—
a predictable pathology for detainees who hate Lieutenant 2,

the more dangerous, the more unconscious, as if the wall
shoved itself against the faces of detainees responsible
for their welcome to America in this way, faces slammed against
a T-shirt THESE COLORS DON'T RUN that the officers
have taped to the sally port, and that Lieutenant 2
videotapes to make sure that the detainees confront

what it means to have their hands "goosenecked," to make a wall
"waltz" with a stripped-searched detainee responsible
for making us act the way we do, you, me, Lieutenant 1 and 2
forced by these detainees to throw off our mental chains and
        confront
star-crossed perplexities amongst our officers:
so welcome to my castle, you fucking terrorist: up against

the wall, don't think I don't know how to make you responsible
for the ways we Lieutenants, both 1 and 2, train our officers
to confront the walls you terrorists love, and love to shove your
        faces against.

THE CHOPPER'S SIDES WERE OPEN TO THE NIGHT AIR, and I instinctively shoved myself back on the bench as far as I could get—not very far, it turned out, certainly not far enough to quell my unease about hurtling through the air with no door in front of me.

The contractor gave me thumbs up, and I at least knew enough to give thumbs up back, and then the chopper blades accelerated faster and louder. He slid the lenses of his night-vision goggles past the lip of his helmet and down over his eyes to keep watch for snipers on the ground, and then we slowly ascended, the nose of the chopper dipping slightly as the tail lifted up, and we soared straight up until the pilot adjusted the pitch of the rotors and we shot ahead, eventually climbing to about a hundred feet over the city.

Everything was dark down below for the first quarter mile, and then we were crossing over Baghdad, the lights of the cars on the road flickering softly, houselights shining in the windows. The pilot occasionally flicked a switch on the instrument panel, and then, as we rose higher, and the night air got very cold, the contractor slid the Lexan-glass doors closed on the passenger part of the tiny cabin. The chopper shimmied back and forth in the light wind, soft buffets, almost the way a child might pet a cat on the head. Just above the pilot's helmet silhouetted against the curved glass of the windshield shimmered another little galaxy. Switches glowing in the darkness, an overhead instrument panel lit up the pilot's hand as he leisurely lifted his left arm from time to time to switch something off or on.

For a moment, I felt immensely happy: I had the reverie of myself as a child, looking up at dayglow stars stuck to the ceiling over my bed—a memory I knew to be false, since I'm way too old for such things to have existed when I was a kid, nor were my parents the type to indulge me with dayglow stars. I knew, even as I took pleasure in it, that my fantasy was out of sync with the reality on the ground, not to mention the contractor hunching forward, his gun in his lap, intently scanning the darkness below. At least the contractor had his orders and his night-vision goggles. What I had to go on was the drone of helicopter noise, its surgical detachment from the neighborhood alleys and streets, and the way my own hypervigilant senses magnified and crystallized the light and dark flow of the city beneath me. One of Saddam's former palaces, encircled by a moat that testified to the dead dictator's love of water, glowed dimly below us, looking like an Arabian Nights fantasy in bad taste, and reputed to have a torture chamber in the basement. Aloft in the chopper and looking down, I found and continue to find it hard to know what tone to take when the truth is both atrocious and banal.

And if you were on the ground looking up? In an oral history of the Iraq War, I'd come across this account of a pregnant woman, Rana Abdul Mahdi, who lives in Sadr City:

> ". . . I saw a helicopter floating very high in the air away from me, and I watched as it fired a rocket toward me and my little sister, Zahra. She was eight. I felt heat all over my body, and then I was on the ground as the street filled with smoke. There were bodies all around me, and I saw my sister with all her insides spilling out her front. She was reaching for me, motioning with her hand for me to come and help. . . . I saw my left foot was gone. It was sitting there in the street a little ways from me."

UH-IN

The light lift "Huey" rose from the floor of night
into the darkness of the brain
where it felt the sullen winds pushing it this way and that,

following the current of a thought
into a blankness and far-seeingness
that, as I rose in the actual chopper, released me

to confront the scabbard of Orion's belt.
Behind him the scorpion menaced his exposed heel.
But then the rotor roar filled up the space between night sky

and ground-dark.
The imagination slipped down over my eyes
like a pair of night-vision goggles: what they showed me

was myself strapped in, staring down at Baghdad
at one of Saddam's kitsch palaces
that looked like something out of *The Thousand and One Nights*

in which only Scheherazade's unending flight of words
to keep the sultan from murdering her
can preserve her from his scimitar.

How picturesque the imagination
envisions the storied world lit up by infrared.
How the helicopter's retracted doors letting in the cold night air

refreshed and restored the sultan in me
while putting under threat of death
the insurgent imagination that thinks it can talk its way

out of the void it hovers in, its blades rendered
an invisible blur as it holds its position
in the darkness, intent on the levitating heaviness

that allows it to convince itself, suspended
in the air,
that it's really weightless.

ON OUR WAY BACK FROM ONE MISSION IN BAGHDAD, I learned that a suicide bomber had gotten inside the Green Zone, or what since the US troop withdrawal in 2011 had been rechristened the International Zone—the IZ, as the locals put it. That meant the rest of the city qualified as the Red Zone. But the Red Zone, the IZ, no matter—sure enough, a day later, the bomber blew himself up not too far away from where we'd just conducted a workshop.

But such incidents, after the workshop with Mariam, now took on a subtly different quality. I had begun to feel such rage about the relentlessness of the killing, the zealotry that could inspire it, the religious mania that seemed to brutalize people into killing other ordinary Iraqis who most likely weren't particularly religious, except as a formal, societal, or familial instinct, and who had no doctrinal grudge against anyone. Their only sin was to be in the wrong place at the wrong time. But since Mariam's story, written and read with such understated feeling, my rage, and the comfort it gave me because of my certainty that it was justified, could never take hold of me without also seeing the image of her brother, gently, very gently, bending down to kiss his sister, to ask her if she needed anything at the market, and whispering, again with the utmost gentleness, that this would be the last time he would ever see her.

4

Homage to Vallejo

1/ INTENSITY AND HEIGHT

I want to write, but only foam comes out,
I want to say so much but it's all crap—
there aren't any numbers left that can't be added up,
nobody writes down pyramids without meaning it.

I want to write, but I've got a puma's brains;
I want to crown myself with laurel, but it stinks of onions.
There's no word spoken that doesn't dissolve in mist,
there's no god and no son of god, only progress.

So come on, to hell with it, let's go eat weeds,
eat the flesh and fruit of our stupid
tears and moans, of our pickled melancholy souls.

Come on! Let's go! So what if I'm wounded—let's go
drink what's already been drunk,
let's go, crow, and find another crow to fuck.

2/ HAT, COAT, GLOVES

Right in front of the Comédie-Française
is the Regency Café; and right inside it, there's this room, hidden,
with a table and an easy chair. When I go in,
house dust, already on its feet, stands motionless.

Between my lips made of rubber, a cigarette butt
smoulders, and in the smoke you can see two intensive
smokes, the café's thorax, and in that
thorax an oxide of elemental grief.

It matters that autumn grafts itself into other autumns,
it matters that autumn merges into young shoots,
the cloud into half-years, cheekbones into a wrinkle.

It's crucial to smell like a madman who spouts
theories about how hot snow is, how fugitive the turtle,
the "how" how easy, how deadly the "when."

3/ BEST CASE

Look, at the very best, I'm someone other—
some guy who walks around marble statues, who enters
his adult clay into indexes of blood, and feels
the rage and fear of the fox chased to its hole—

and if someone anoints my shoulders
with indigoes of mercy, I'll declare
to my absent soul that there's no hellishly
paradisal elsewhere for me to go.

And if they try to choke me on the sea's wafer,
telling me it tastes like His flesh, more acid
than sweet, like Kant's notions of truth, I'll cough

it all up: *No, never!* I'm other as a germ, a satanic
tubercle, a moral ache in a plesiosaur's molar:
in my posthumous suspicions, all bets are off!

4/ ANOTHER DAY OF LIFE

I'll die in my apartment on a cold bright day,
with nobody around, the apartment next door gone
dead still while wind shushes through the balcony,
though the branches somehow aren't moving, just as the sun

doesn't move, everything's so quiet, so frozen.
Parked cars, plastic bags bleached in the bare trees,
a couple of those Mylar balloons tied to a chair on
the balcony next door, celebrating something, maybe?

. . . now sagging listless on the floor,
as if every last molecule had been pierced by a needle—
Tom Sleigh is dead, he stared up into the air,

the sky was pale blue as usual and he couldn't feel
the cold coming through the window, and there wasn't
much to say or not say—and nobody, anyway, to say or not say it.

5/ MY JAILER WON'T WEEP TO BE MY LIBERATOR

My cell's four walls, whitening in the sun,
keep counting one another—but their number
never changes, despite my jailer's
innumerable keys to chains

wrenching the nerves to their extremities.
The two longer walls hurt me more—who knows why—
their salt-stained cracks like two mothers who die
after labor, but give birth to twin boys

whose hands they still hold. And here I am,
all alone, with just my right hand to make do
for both hands, raising it high into

the air to search for the third arm
that between my where and my when
will father this crippled coming of age of a man.

6/ INSOMNIA IS THE ONLY PRAYER LEFT

How childish is the spectacle of the stained
glass's holiness: the night doesn't give a shit what
goes on inside human beings, the night
has its own web of dendrites refuting the inane

prayers prayed for the dying, for the confessions
going on between earthworms and earth, between
the way a man argues with his own shoulder bones.
All the while, barracudas in a coral canyon,

a sea turtle flying, swim through fathoms
and fathoms of images that keep crashing
on the shore of the eye that never shuts—

and smarts in its sleeplessness staring
up into the dark shadowed by stingrays, gas stations,
the slow flapping wing of a lottery ticket.

Global Warming Fugue

Sitting outdoors in perfect fall weather, waiting
       for the waiter
inside to see me, I've put on my mask of *No-worries! No-way-scared!*
       that now starts to slip
—it's dumb to think of water rising and sandbags holding
       a plastic tarp
in place against waves onrushing that won't ever stop
       slapping against
plate glass, the fear so intense it's almost like my dream
       of silence
when I can't move a muscle and the taxi
       runs me down—
the iced tea in my glass sweats in crystal-beaded rivulets
       but it's such perfect weather
who can think of global warming? But I did, I do,
       I went online
and tried to find the places on earth where,
       when all the shit
comes down in the next twenty or thirty years, it might be
       OK to live—
there goes that woman again, talking to her brown mutt
       she thinks is so cute
she stops almost every time she sees me sitting at my table,
       "Isn't he the cutest little bug,"
the bug-eyed Pekingese with the long brown fur darkening
       to sable at the tips
looking oddly mongoloid, though really pretty friendly,
       "Yes, cute" is all I
can ever manage, though now she's off to the next table
       where some college girls

don't mind that liver-colored tongue licking them: ugh!
      But so what, live and let live,
Mr. Fussy should just relax and go back to his doomsday:
      apparently, Great Britain
is a good place to live out global warming because the land mass
      of an island not too big
will still be temperate enough in the interior to benefit
      from the ocean's moderating
influence: first time I ever thought of the ocean
      as moderating: I used to surf
in it, and get high before paddling out to get knocked
      off my board in a thousand ways—
man, I was no Mike Doyle—Mike paddling out about sunset
      just north of the PB pier,
and in his jams a baggie with a match and cigarette—I always
      wanted to have Mike's muscles,
long swimmer's muscles, but rounded and thick
      from years and years
of paddling, his short legs and lithe torso perfect
      for walking up and down
his long board: just as the sun touched the horizon, he'd take out
      his baggie, strike the match
and cup it from whatever wind was left (the wind always
      dies at sunset)
and touch it to his cigarette (a *Camel? Parliament?* I never knew)
      and then wheel
around on his board and paddle hard to catch the swell
      you could see mounding up
under the pier, and when he'd caught the curl and his board
      found an edge and spume
flew back behind him, he'd walk out to the nose and hang ten,
      and take a long slow drag
before letting his hand drift down to his side, where he'd hang
      that way forever, profile
the acme of cool, beautiful, I'd later think, as the statue

of the Winged Victory
at the top of the Louvre's staircase—Mike smoking his cigarette
    mixed with dope,
one hand behind his back, weightless and ineffable as an astronaut,
    chest thrust out,
long hair briny and shining from foam tattering
    as the wave
kept breaking behind him, or barreling on big days
    over his shoulder
so he shot the tube, crouched down inside the green room
    like crouching
inside that old chandelier store so crowded with chandeliers
    you couldn't move two inches
without glass pendants swaying and clinking against
    your head and neck, brushing
against your shoulders, the glass chill, the light diffusing
    all around your head.
All afternoon of Frankenstorm Sandy I walked down
    by the waterfront (my ex-wife
who's right about most things called me a thrill-seeker)
    and watched the water
surging toward shore as the tide rose, swamping the pilings
    over by the River Café
and breasting the ferry landing, gusts of wind tearing
    at the trees' heads
while the East River turned to overlapping scales'
    dull gray and duller silver
that the gusts drove before them, trash whirling in
    eddies against shore,
plastic bottles bobbing madly in scum-froth, driftwood
    with nails glinting
washed at by the tide cresting, the flooding over
    onto concrete
leaving tide-wrack along the waterfront walkways—
    at least the ones

not shut down by metal fences weighed in place
        by sand bags—
though chainlink fences also sagged in the wind and looked
        about to topple
while ailanthus and elms lashed in heady arcs
        that stripped limbs
off branches shedding leaves going yellower
        and yellower
in the fading light contrasting with how gray
        the sky got, the violence
of the storm convulsive, falling silent almost, then whipping up
        even stronger so the wind
pushed you along, then stopped so abruptly my leg muscles
        braced against its force
stumble forward wildly when the wind lets up
        before roaring again
in a movie-Cyclops voice so that I thought more than once
        this is like Cyclops' cave
and I'm trapped here with the crew, though the crew would be
        Sarah and Hannah, both safe
thank God up in Syracuse, and Ed and Lesley safely indoors,
        Ellen up in Providence,
and only me stupid enough to be out: so Cyclops
        starts shouting
that as a special favor, *You, thrill-seeking Mr. Fussy, will be the last*
        among the crew that I devour
and the stoplight above my head suddenly sizzles out
        and I wish I was indoors
or sitting where I am now, drinking my fourth iced tea and I'm
        like a not-so-wily
Ulysses (and just how wily was he anyway, getting himself
        and his men walled up inside
the cave of a giant, hungry, one-eyed cannibal) who has to risk
        his life because he's
trapped inside his own myth, his hero's story that he tells himself

even as Cyclops eats his men,
caught between the monster and his own self-image
        entrapped like greenhouse gases
that have no place to escape to, while what he wants
        to see himself be
here in the traffic noise and calm of fading sunlight
        may just be the guy that's me
who watches reflecting off the window across the street
        and right into my eyes
bright streaks of glare flashing brighter as if the light is a knob
        turning up and up in volume
so that I hear the movie voice start shouting, *Noman is killing me,*
        Noman is killing me!
to which very sensibly the other Cyclops shout,
        Well, if no man
is killing you, stop making all that noise.

From the Ass's Mouth: A Theory of the Leisure Class

Up on stage in the three-quarters empty auditorium,
the lights turned down, up where the auditorium resounded
to *A Midsummer Night's Dream* performed

clumsily by me reading out Bottom's speech when he turns
from an ass back into a human while the rest of the class
sniggered or flirted, sat back and chewed gum,

the words in the auditorium lived out their hour—
and after rehearsal, when I got on my bike, red bike, fat tires,
to pedal home under cottonwood trees, I turned round corners

I'd never seen in our tiny mountain town,
years and years went by, I was still pedaling—
it wasn't a dream except maybe in the way logic works in dreams—

I had two heads now, my ass's head, my human head,
my ass's bray more eloquent than my human bray
of wonder at my change: *The eye of man hath not heard,*

the ear of man hath not seen . . . my stumbling
tongue piecing through Shakespeare's
bitter oratory about *no bottom* to Bottom's dream . . .

I put my bike in the carport and started throwing
a tennis ball against the brick wall, thinking
over and over, *no bottom no bottom*—

the harder I threw, the more the words
weren't mine, the ball smashing brick
while there in the auditorium the words

were like a taunt, like Theseus's
taunts spoken behind my back because I was just
an ass, not Duke of Athens: but after the play, the cast

gave me the *papier-maché*
ass's head and I kept it first in the room I shared
with my two brothers, putting it on to sniff

the dried glue, feel the claustrophic fit, and stumble
half-blind to the bathroom mirror where I looked
out at myself through holes in the muzzle,

the ass's painted on eyes and lips what people saw
when they saw me, Shakespeare's words booming
back from the head's suffocating hollows

coming straight from the ass's mouth, not mine.
I don't remember how, but it ended in an alcove
above the carport where it softened

on the chicken wire, the paper sagged
and began to flake away, the muzzle and the eye-holes
shriveling into a gray, ulcerous mass—

when we moved from that town it got thrown
into the trash, taken to the dump and burned:
onion eaters, garlic eaters, hard-handed men,

that's what Bottom and the mechanicals were—
and that's what I was, what I've always been,
riding along on my bike's fat tires

while that half god half man Theseus
laughs his courteous contempt of us whose
words come out like a tangled chain—which is

why there's no bottom, why there's never been
a bottom if you're just an ass who speaks prose
to the Duke's verse—an ass who kissed the Queen

of the Shadows and never got over it, my long,
scratchy ears and hairy muzzle pressed
to the ethereal, immortal, almost-not-thereness of her skin.

Stairway

In those days, so many stairways were said to lead to happiness, mainly of a sexual kind—and as I climbed those stairs, I could hear my name being called from the top, as I so often did back then—and the sight of me bolting up the stairs with my eager, cartoon tongue hanging out wasn't as sad or silly as it might seem. Naturally, there were the avatars of sex, the ones who claimed to hate it, the others who thought it led to universal harmony—they were out in front of the rest of us, and they believed it, and so did I: but as a friend recently said to me, *Always having to lead the way, be in front of the troops, all those speeches and sermons and truths you'd have to tell: such a burden.* It went on like this, stairway branching into stairway, endless others going up or down to meetings just as I was. And after many years, there we were: to find you, to hold you, led like steps up and down . . . the sadness and silliness, though just as sad and silly, were somehow more in earnest. Even my doggy-dog instincts, strong as always, understood some reckoning was at hand. The two of us had decided, mutually and irrevocably, to start climbing a stair that we knew was partly ruined, unlit except by the capriciousness of moonlight. But we had a method—and until the day when one or both of us stumbled off into the nothingness below, we committed ourselves to it—when one said, *Left,* we turned left. Which meant, because I have a terrible sense of direction, that I went whichever way you went.

The Negative

Back in those days, when he told me about his adventures
in sex clubs it wasn't the whys and wherefores

but technical details, like going rafting
down the Colorado River; and when he wrote

about a gay male friend whose first sexual experience
was with his stepfather, the friend told him

it wasn't weird, but the best possible thing
that could have happened . . . I saw then that God,

who I never believed in, was dwelling in my heart
as a negative: that the negative had been developed

into a picture of a man who stares up at the sky
on a day so clear he sees through the mountain's shadows

to the divinely human-seeming form that climbs it—
a neighbor in running shoes and sunglasses

jogging up the slope with his dog, tongue panting
and slavering, an acute look of happiness in its eyes

that could turn at any moment into exhaustion or pain
as in a maze of cubicles called Asshole Alley, little pyramids

of canvas called Lust of the Pharaohs, different pricing
for what you want, depending on the equipment,

the air thick with a sour, acidic, head-fogging reek
of come. . . . And my pal the poet, who believed

in infernal chemistry, in the spirit as a kind
of "spooky action at a distance," he communed

with this God, this eternally dying father of all matter
who made out of our bodies his own maze of cubicles

where he hides himself away—his sanctuary
Asshole Alley where God's own unholy loves

bubble all around him like a cauldron in his ears—
and my poet pal heard the bubbling, he stirred

the pot, he showed me the holy city, the sexual New Jerusalem
that came prepared as a bride adorned for her husband . . .

—That was how it was in those days, back when my friend
hadn't yet met the coroner who wrote down

his cause of death as "polysubstance abuse"
that brought on his heart attack while fucking . . .

And regardless if I believed, whenever
we were together God shone clearer—

those were the days when every morning God woke up
in a blur of ecstasy and went to bed every night

in divine rage. Whoever loved him,
he loved. Whoever hated him,

he hated back: for who can doubt the vitality
of hate or the volatility of love.

Party at Marquis de Sade's Place

It's like you're looking over my shoulder
and saying, as I sway on my third drink at the party
while a woman with pink hair and pierced upper lip
tells me how she did her piercings herself, it's like
you're saying, *Hey man, why are you still here*
instead of putting a gun to your head like I did?
Your voice is broomstraw, wispy, shattered,
sweeping away the woman's voice who presses
on a scar dead center on her sternum and says, *This*
hurts, I used to have a piercing here—the light's so sharp
I can see beneath her silk blouse's sheer scalloped
edges a tiny patch of skin she rubs more raw, maybe

flirting but maybe not, both of us in our
bodies brushing up against limits that dare
us to go further, but also just doing what people
at parties do, nothing not allowed—and is that why,
my friend, you've come back, lonely maybe,
wanting to burst in with advice for what I
should say to her?—but neither of us is really
in this moment of this woman and me talking
but in this moment where your voice comes from rubble
on the mountain framed by the stone arch I'm
looking through, you're saying, smiling,
Tom, I wanted to go out at the top of my game,

with good shoes on my feet, you know how much
good shoes and a suit, you know how much
all of that costs? And as she and I stand talking
right there at the actual Marquis de Sade's
actual chateau that Pierre Cardin has bought to add
to his collection of four hundred chateaux, all of it
so ridiculously unlikely that I start to see your point,
I say as a way of flirting you'd applaud,
So how's the old Marquis treating you? and she, smiling
back at me with her pierced lip says, *Sadistically.*
But now you're telling me how some aristocrat stood
gazing from the death cart with undistracted eyes

at the sights of Paris, the crowds gathered on the sides
of the streets no longer blocking the view so
for the first/last time he saw the buildings, windows
of houses he'd visited and got drunk in, as I'm
staring now though my stare's nothing like your condemned
man's blinking, infinite leisure—*So fuck it,* you said,
that's how I decided to go out, looking
at it straight, OK? And then I'm back talking
to her pierced lip while I watch you watch me play the fool
by staring up into the sun in its million
million years of never breaking down—
though just by shutting my eyes I can make the sun fall.

ER

Don't look behind you is what I remember telling myself,
scared in the prison opening all around me,
for encircling me were tiers of cells and walkways

in a circle leading up to the skylit dome where a dozen birds
whirled among the Russian prisoners you could visit by paying
a few rubles. They dressed in black uniforms, wore flat black caps

and pushed mops and buckets in front of their black boots,
the slopping water driving a mouse down the corridor,
mops leaving a slick of soap drying on stone floors.

When the doors closed behind me, I could hear
the room I'd been in go silent and the room I was entering
grow louder—and then there weren't any more prisoners,

no white nights, there was just me and the triage nurse
and my urine sample—black—what have I done wrong
or what has gone wrong and what more is

going wrong before it can't be helped? And then a Mr. Mohammed,
from Queens, one foot amputated, the other an open wound
wound in bandages, began to shout, despite his diabetes,

Bring me my apple juice! I am a son of Prince Abdullah!
And the nurse brought him a little juice box
but asked him about sugar, should he be drinking sugar,

and he told her apple juice was fine, it was orange juice
that was bad as she quieted him down
by patting his arm—but then he started shouting, *Ice! Ice!*—

what kind of hospital is this that you don't give us ice?
And so she brought him ice and quieted him
down by patting his arm, until he asked her in a voice

that already knew the answer, *Do you think my foot
stinks? Tell me what you smell.* But despite the smell,
and despite the old man groaning in the bed next

to mine, his smashed hip still unnumbed by morphine, Dilaudid,
even OxyContin, while his daughter keeps pleading
with him, saying, so gently, for what seems like hours, *Dad,*

please, you have to keep covered up—despite the metronomic
drip of the IV in my arm, the contrapuntal
beep of the heart monitors, my panic

begs me to let it go—I'm not going to die, am I? No, not
this time, maybe another, my mind skittering off
into crevices and corners to sniff out

some crumbs left by one of the prisoners who so tames me
that I creep into his hand to eat out of his palm—and when
I finally do die, he'll put me in a cigarette pack and lay me

under the cross in the exercise yard in the insomniac white nights,
while over the wall, littering the parking lot, lie hundreds of messages
the prisoners write on paper scraps they fold into darts

and through toilet paper rolls joined painstakingly
together into long blowguns, blow out
through the barred windows to be picked up by

what must be mothers, sisters, girlfriends since all of them
are women unfolding and reading and putting
the messages in their purses, ready to send them on

to the address written inside, until they get tired
of reading and leave the rest unread, glinting
under arc lights, each crisp fold relaxing in the summer air.

Scroll

Just as in the movie about Hitler's brain, in which Hitler
has himself decapitated and his head placed, still living,
in what looks like a fish tank, so that after

Germany's defeat he can rise again
with the special G gas and rule the world
from South America,

and just as the the dread of watching Hitler's skin,
clearly made of wax, begin to melt off the skull
as the movie ends and the credits roll

and flames shoot up around his head
so that everything that should have remained
secret, hidden, has become visible,

and just as Bill Freed, the actor who played Hitler,
never acted again, his dialogue consisting
of yelling, *Mach schnell! Mach schnell!*

while his flesh and moustache burn,
yes, just as the name "Station Zed" in the actual camp
of Sachsenhausen a few miles beyond Berlin,

on a casual Sunday in hot July,
turns out to be an *SS* joke—you came in at Gate A
and went out by Station Zed—so the tape hiss

of the survivor's German, digitized down
but not erased to give that feel of *This
is real,* then overlaid by the translator's English

that becomes garbled background to the camp walls,
so that hiss turns into an echo, an echo
of an echo in the voice telling

how "Iron Gustav plunged among us
to beat us with a pipe, his slaver flying in our faces,
his hunched-over body and dark complexion

nothing like an Aryan's," so all these
echoes and counter-echoes drifting
and unraveling under birch and poplar trees

in the nowhere breeze in the shady cemetery
slowly entangle and blur
into the *caw caw   caw caw*

that rises up where clouds in Technicolor light
turn to an ancient parchment scroll, some mystical notation
summoning pure evil, though really just voices

you didn't expect to hear, your mother's voice
calling, calling you back home, or the dead lover
you abandoned and haven't thought about in years,

your own brain's canned footage,
their faces like notes that eddy and flow,
whispers and murmurings of fear and dread . . .

and then strings playing so softly the notes barely graze your ears
as you stand before the gates of Station Zed—
not to see the dead of invisible worlds

but to hear this melody
stolen from another horror movie,
The Creature from the Black Lagoon, begin to play.

Proof of Poetry

I wanted first to end up as a drunk in the gutter
and in my twenties I almost ended up there—

and then as an alternative to vodka, to live

alone like a hermit philosopher and court
the extreme poverty that I suspected lay in store for me anyway—

and then there were the years in which

I needed very badly to take refuge in mediocrity,
years like blunt scissors cutting out careful squares,

and that was the worst, the very worst—

you could say that always my life
was like a patchwork quilt always ripped apart—

my life like scraps stitched together in a dream

in which animals and people,
plants, chimeras, stars,

even minerals were in a preordained harmony—

a dream forgotten because it has to be forgotten,
but that I looked for desperately, but only sporadically

found in fragments, a hand lifted to strike

or caress or simply lifted for some unknown reason—
and in memory too, some specific pain, sensation of cold or warmth.

I loved that harmony in all its stages of passion,

the voices still talking inside me . . . but then, instead of harmony,
there was nothing but rags scattered on the ground.

And maybe that's all it means to be a poet.

Dogcat Soul

To be hollowed out night by night,
to feel this continuum between envy
and desire, to have the kind of fur that sheds
sparks in the bedroom's shifting dark,
to sense, when I'm asleep, your whiskers
measuring the void around my face
that expands inexorably year by year,
to know that in your eyes God is just a bird
trapped in the burning bush, and to have
to disappoint you with my dogcat soul,
more dog than cat, really, more nakedly
beseeching, less able than you to be
out there on your own, given all that,
what makes you crave my touch tonight?
When your eyes entrap me, I splinter
into your looking, into what your looking
sees, the seeing itself stripping me down
to flesh and bone, and found wanting—
my face gone vagrant, paralyzed in your pupils
yet heightened and varnished beyond fact:
I fall, am falling, I've plummeted beyond
the frame, no internal balance-wheel to land me
on all fours, no mechanism of grace,
no safe harbor under the radiant
engine block, the streets rippling with black ice.
But don't turn away from me: turn my skinhead
to furhead, teach me slash, slink, creep.
Show me how to survive under a heating vent.

Prayer for Recovery

The cursor moving back along the line erases what was was.
What was keeps existing under Edit so that all you need to do is
click Undo. So much of time gets lived out that way—
at the momentary center of the line erasing.

When I push my IV pole down the dark, glass hall, the droplets'
atavistic sheen drips into my veins with an absolute weight as if
the bag of potassium chloride, hanging in sovereign judgment
above my head, assures me that justice, death or life,

will be done. And though it's not for me to understand,
when I cross the beam that throws open the door so silently
and swiftly, it makes me want to think that like these rivets fastening

glass to iron, some state of me that was will go on,
either as the will of some will that isn't mine, or out of mercy,
or from the contract between the rivet gun and some unseen hand.

Second Sight

In my fantasy of fatherhood, in which I'm
your real father, not just the almost dad
arriving through random channels of divorce,
you and I don't lie to one another—
shrugging each other off when words
get the best of us but coming
full circle with wan smiles.
When you hole up inside yourself,
headphones and computer screen
taking you away, I want to feel in ten years
that if I'm still alive you'll still look
at me with that same wary expectancy,
your surreptitious cool-eyed appraisal
debating if my love for you is real.
Am I destined to be those shark-faced waves
that my death will one day make you enter?
You and your mother make such a self-sufficient pair—
in thrift stores looking for your prom dress,
what father could stand up to your unsparing eyes
gauging with such erotic calculation
your figure in the mirror? Back of it all, when I
indulge my second sight, all I see are dead zones:
no grandchildren, no evenings at the beach, no bonfires
in a future that allows one glass of wine
per shot of insulin. Will we both agree
that I love you, always, no matter
my love's flawed, aging partiality?
My occupation now is to help you be alone.

Songs for the End of the World

I

On the other side of praise
it's time to chop down the tall tree in the ear—

enough enough with the starlit promontories—

a nervous condition traces itself
in lightning in the clouds,
a little requiem rattles among Coke cans
and old vegetable tins

and shifts into a minor key
blowing through the dying ailanthus,

grieving to the beat beginning to pour down

percussive as a run
on a nomad's flute of bone
while a car engine dangling from a hoist and chain
sways in a translucent gown of rain.

2

Where does it go when it's all gone?
Coleridge's son, Hartley,
wants to know what would be left if all the men and women,
and trees, and grass, and birds and beasts,
and sky and ground were all gone:
everything just darkness and coldness
but nothing to be dark and cold.

Which was what my father
imagined all the time,
calculating with his slide rule the missile's
drag and lift, as he smeared
across the paper the equation's
figures propelling his pencil lead
into the void.

3

And after splashdown, what?
An emptiness like an empty subway car
stumbled into by mistake

on a drunken night
turning into
morning

with the world
stretching out
like wind walking on a lake?—

the body wavering, almost
disappearing
into the inside-outness of being

in that emptiness, its peaks and valleys
and absolute stillness?

4

His shadow anchored to a semi's tires,
down there with the mussels, oysters, a starfish even
that twice a day shine up through oily film
where river meets sea meets river.

And I can track him in the sonar
of dolphin, seal
as if his pencil
hit the sea floor

echoing everywhere
filling the sea's room,
unstringing the current's loom

in which warp
and weft unravel
into oscilloscoping wave.

5

"He began to think of making
a moving image
of what never stops moving
that would bring order

to eternal being,
and so make movement move
according to number—which, of course, Socrates,
is what we call time . . .

And so he brought into being the Sun, the Moon,
and five other stars, for Time must begin.
These he called wanderers, and they stand guard

over the numbers of time—and human beings are so forgetful,
they don't realize that time
is really the wandering of these bodies."

6

An all-morning downpour shadowy
as the stained insides of his coffee cup.
He didn't look up, didn't talk,
didn't rush me to the car, but gave his head

the slightest inclination.
We sat while the news talked on and on,
each of us glad to sink down into ourselves,
to not have to speak: it was enough, more than enough

to know the other knew we could settle
in that silence, and no vow or spoken understanding
would be as strong.

And all we did as we sat there driving along
was move from that point where everything originates
until point to point the line we made together got drawn.

7

The abandoned pit-house sliding down the cliff
sliding into the sea
is lost in fog
wrapped around

the headland's scree—
and in the mine's undersea tunnel
where miners walk out (along with my father's father's ghosts)
a mile or more under the waves

you can sense the old imperatives like played-out veins of tin
shining up for the men
walking briskly to their unsuspected

deaths, while just above their heads, a moment before the cave-in,
they can hear, as always, boulders rolling on the seafloor,
a job of work to do before the next shift.

8

"I am a dreaming & therefore
an indolent man—.
I am a starling self-incaged,
and always in the Moult,

and my whole Note is Tomorrow,
& tomorrow, & tomorrow . . ."
Which because it was how he felt
it's what he wrote.

But now there's no tomorrow,
only languor and despondency.
And under that shelter in the storm, among rocks

falling, he finally felt free
to say what his Daemon made him say, and looked up into the rain
and was for that instant washed clean.

9

English letters are Greek ones dried up.
The aurora on the screen
pulses more real than real.
The post-nuclear, post-holocaust rain he tried to understand
is only another afternoon when the world ends.

And now what passes through him
is a windchime ringing, casting parabolic shadows on the ground
as he hunches at work in his little cubicle,
a cell 8 x 10
which is just another world coming to an end

when twenty years on since the chiming ceased,
I try again to understand the points he plots
where thrust equals gravity and drag
so the rocket can keep soaring on forever.

10

Glowing on the screen, the initial
capital in the shape of Omega holds inside its void
two flying dragons biting their own tails.

And on another page
Alpha traces out the lines
of the Tower of Babel collapsing.

And just beneath that, a king lies dreaming of a golden statue
crushed by a stone that becomes a great mountain
so that the four kingdoms, gold, silver, brass, iron,

shine in gilt from the vellum—
and across Daniel's face the shadow of a wing
which is the Lord's wing whispering to Daniel the dream of the king

turns black as the screen when the screen goes to sleep
and a hand writes an unknown equation across the dark.

Valediction

The backyard lives of cat and bird
and the way leaves give themselves
away this instant to the all-but-no breeze
creeping across the silver-painted roof where clouds,

reflected, pass dark, then bright
above a book left out by the vacant deck chair
fluttering its pages, signaling to the reader somewhere out of sight
to come back, come back and start the book over,

this all arrives without a valediction forbidding anything,
just the sense of seeing something
or someone for the last time: the poet's faded fedora

in a tea-store window haunting this October's primary
blues bringing back mid-May and the missing mate
of the nightingale singing "day long and night late."

i.m. Seamus Heaney

"The Craze"

Demmies is short for "demolition experts."

"Hunger"

Ba, Akh, and *Duat* are terms used in the Egyptian *Book of the Dead. Ba* is a spiritual entity, often depicted as a human-headed bird hovering over the deceased's body, or exiting the tomb. It's the part of the soul that can travel between the worlds of the living and the dead. *Akh* is the "blessed or 'transfigured' soul" of a dead person whose soul has been judged to be just by Osiris and so is allowed to enter the Afterlife. *Duat* is the dangerous landscape of the underworld, complete with demons and monsters who guard the gates that the *Ba* has to pass through in becoming an *Akh.*

"Eclipse"

A *panga* is a bush knife shaped much like a machete.

A *matatu* is a minibus used as an inexpensive, shared taxi by most ordinary people in Nairobi. They are often decorated with pictures of movie stars, musicians, politicians, and other famous people, as well as religious leaders. They are often equipped with sound systems that blare Motown, R & B, and Afro-Pop.

"KM4"

KM4 refers to a central roundabout in Mogadishu, Somalia, near the Ministry of Education building where a suicide bomber, on October 4, 2011, killed 100 people and injured more than 110 others.

A *macawis* is a sarong-like garment worn by men.

A *chador* is a long robe worn by Muslim women.

UNHCR stands for United Nations High Commissioner for Refugees.

"Proof of Poetry"

The poem is indebted to a passage from Aleksander Wat's *My Century*.

ACKNOWLEDGMENTS

Agni : "Party at Marquis de Sade's Place"
The American Poetry Review: "The Negative"
Blackbird: "KM4"
The Commons: "The Eclipse"
The Cortland Review: "ER," "Hunger"
Five Points: "Homage to Zidane" (under the title, "World Cup"),
    "Refugee Camp"
The New Yorker: "Homage to Mary Hamilton," "A Short History of
    Communism and the Enigma of Surplus Value"
Plume: "From the Ass's Mouth: A Theory of the Leisure Class,"
    "Stairway," "Proof of Poetry"
Poem-a-Day, poets.org, Academy of American Poets: "The Parallel
    Cathedral"
Poetry: "Homage to Vallejo," "The Animals in the Zoo Don't Seem
    Worried," "Homage to Bashō" (published, in a different version,
    under the title, "Six Trees and Two White Dogs . . . Doves?")
Raritan: "Valediction," "Songs for the Cold War," "Prayer for
    Recovery"
The Threepenny Review: "Second Sight"
Tikkun: "Songs for the End of the World"
Tin House: "The Craze," "The Twins"
The Village Voice: "Dogcat Soul," "Global Warming Fugue"
The Yale Review: "'Let Thanks Be Given to the Raven as Is Its Due'"

My thanks to the American Academy of Arts and Letters for the
generous support provided by the John Updike Award, and to Alan,
Michael, and Josh for their encouragement and criticism.

Tom Sleigh is the author of nine collections of poetry, including *Army Cats* and *Space Walk,* winner of the Kingsley Tufts Poetry Award; a collection of essays, *Interview with a Ghost;* and a translation of Euripides' *Herakles.* He has won the Shelley Prize from the Poetry Society of America, an Academy of Arts and Letters Award in Literature, and grants and awards from the Guggenheim Foundation, the National Endowment for the Arts, and the Lila Wallace Fund. He is a Distinguished Professor at Hunter College, where he teaches in the MFA Program. Recently, Sleigh has been traveling as a journalist in Iraq, Iran, Libya, Somalia, and elsewhere. He lives in Brooklyn, New York.

Book design by Connie Kuhnz. Composition by BookMobile Design and Publishing Services, Minneapolis, Minnesota. Manufactured by Versa Press on acid-free, 30 percent postconsumer wastepaper.